THE CHEESE CUTTER

THE EGGY ONE

SILENT-BUT-DEADLY

GASEOUS EMISSION

STINKY FOOD GHOST

TOOT SALUTE

For every reader who has ever farted
(and especially for Mike and Leo Barton, my favorite people)

With huge thanks to Dr. Austin Campbell, science educator and researcher,
who has done lots of research into the creation and composition of human farts!

VIKING
An imprint of Penguin Random House LLC
1745 Broadway, New York, New York 10019

First published in the United States of America by Viking, an imprint of Penguin Random House LLC, 2025

Visit us online at PenguinRandomHouse.com.

Library of Congress Cataloging-in-Publication Data is available.

ISBN 9780593693773

1 3 5 7 9 10 8 6 4 2

Manufactured in China
TOPL

Edited by Meriam Metoui

The artwork in this book was created using ink and Beam Handmade Watercolor paints
(which are sustainable and altogether rad) on paper, alongside Photoshop CC. The main text was
lettered with a well-loved bamboo calligraphy pen and ink. Innumerable cups of tea were
consumed in the process.

I'M TRYING to Love ~~FARTS~~ FLATULENCE

Fixed it!

WORDS & PICTURES by
bethany bARTon

VIKING

As long as there have been people, there have been farts. Farting can be defined as the release of intestinal gas, often as a result of digestion.

And as long as there have been farts, they've been hilarious!

Yup! The oldest recorded joke dates back to 1900 BC, and it's a fart joke! It comes from ancient Sumeria and it's about farting on someone.

HA HA HA HA

Will you stop doing that? You're going to stink up the whole book!

Because that is hilarious.

toot!

Thankfully, being the scientist I am,
I hypothesized my brother might do this.

So I invented the FartFan5000™ to
blow any stinky flatulence out of here.

Quick! *cough* *cough*
Press the button so we
can all breathe again!

Farts have a couple of sources.
Some of our farts come from swallowing air.
We can swallow air when we eat
too quickly or talk while eating.

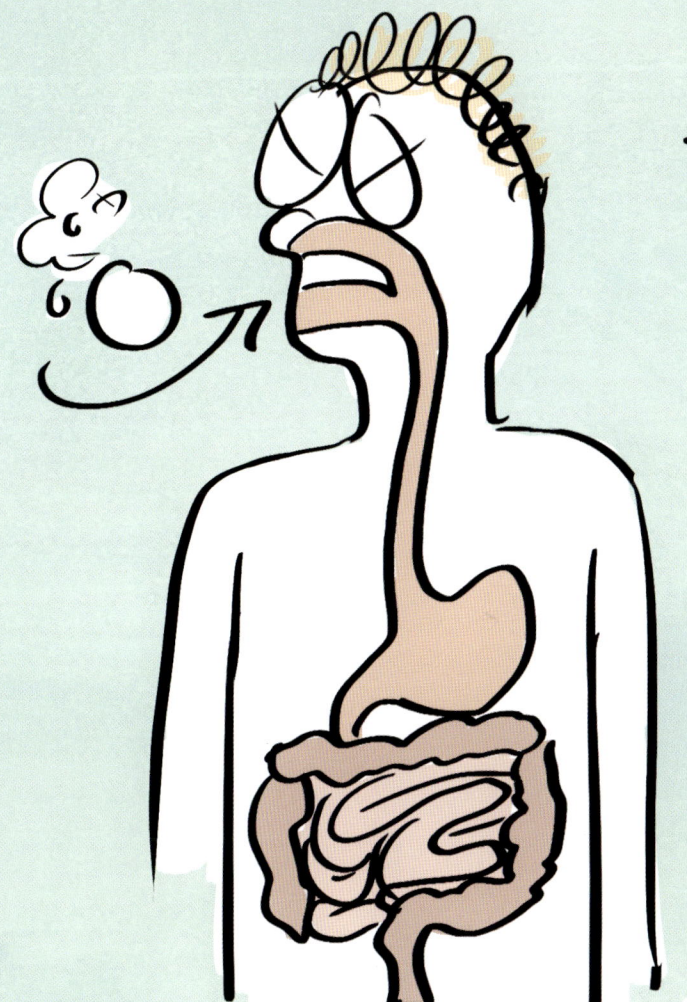

That air goes down into our digestive
tract instead of into our lungs.

And then it's
gotta come out?
In burps or farts?

Exactly!

Farts also come from a much
tinier source: the microorganisms
(aka "microbes") living in our gut.

And when I say
"GUT," I mean our
gastrointestinal system.

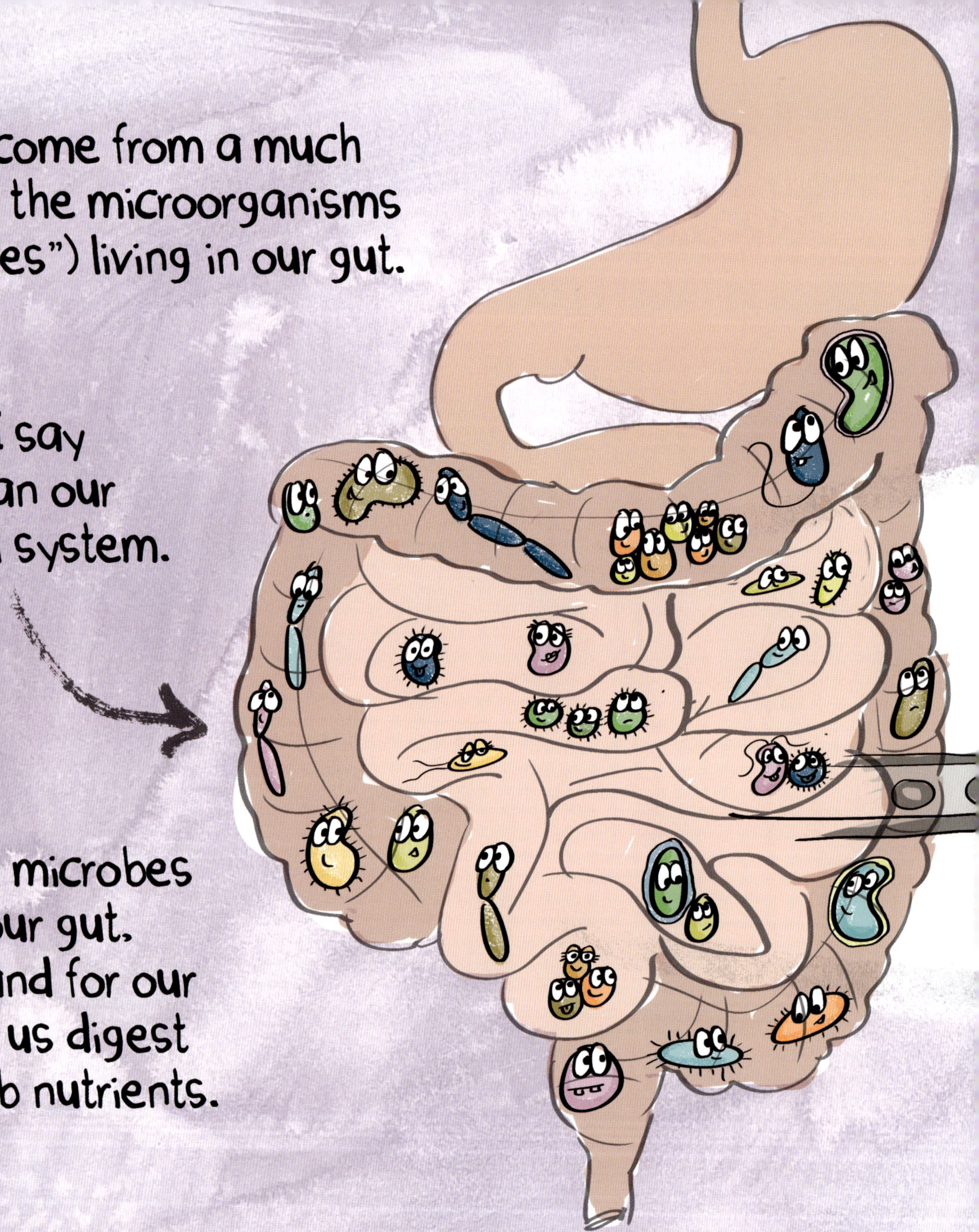

Trillions of tiny microbes
live inside our gut,
working with and for our
bodies to help us digest
food and absorb nutrients.

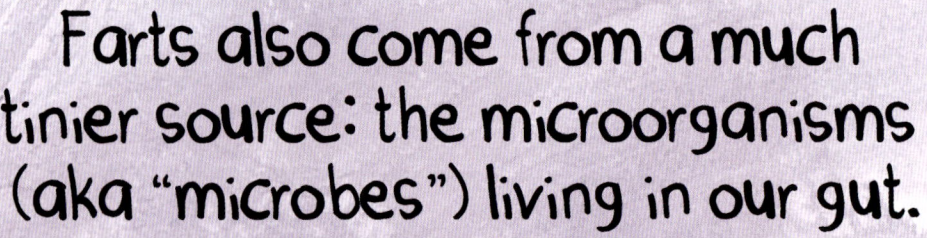

Microbes have been doing this helpful work
for us as long as there have been people!
They are big helpers for healthy digestion.

And when they break down certain foods . . . they release gas.

You can watch this sort of thing
in action by baking bread at home.

When a microbe called yeast
is added to your dough,
it eats up sugars and releases
a gas called carbon dioxide.

here we go!

yay!

sugars!

yum!

This gas fills up the dough,
causing it to expand and rise,

which creates a
fluffy loaf of bread!

Does this mean I'm just . . . a delivery service for trillions of germ farts?

I mean, not exactly?

KEEP UP THE GOOD WORK IN THERE, TINY FART FACTORY WORKERS!

I'm going to ignore that and explain what farts are made of . . .

Oh, that's easy. Farts are the ghosts of my food. Angry food ghosts. Everyone knows that.

What? How did you . . . ? Who is telling you this stuff?!

FART FACTORY DELIVERY!

cough *cough*
That smells . . . terrible.

Someone, please!
cough *cough*
The FartFan5000™!
ON
FF5000
It's . . . our only hope!
gasp

Whew! Okay, back to the science part!
Farts are made up of several different gases.
And get this: every fart is different.

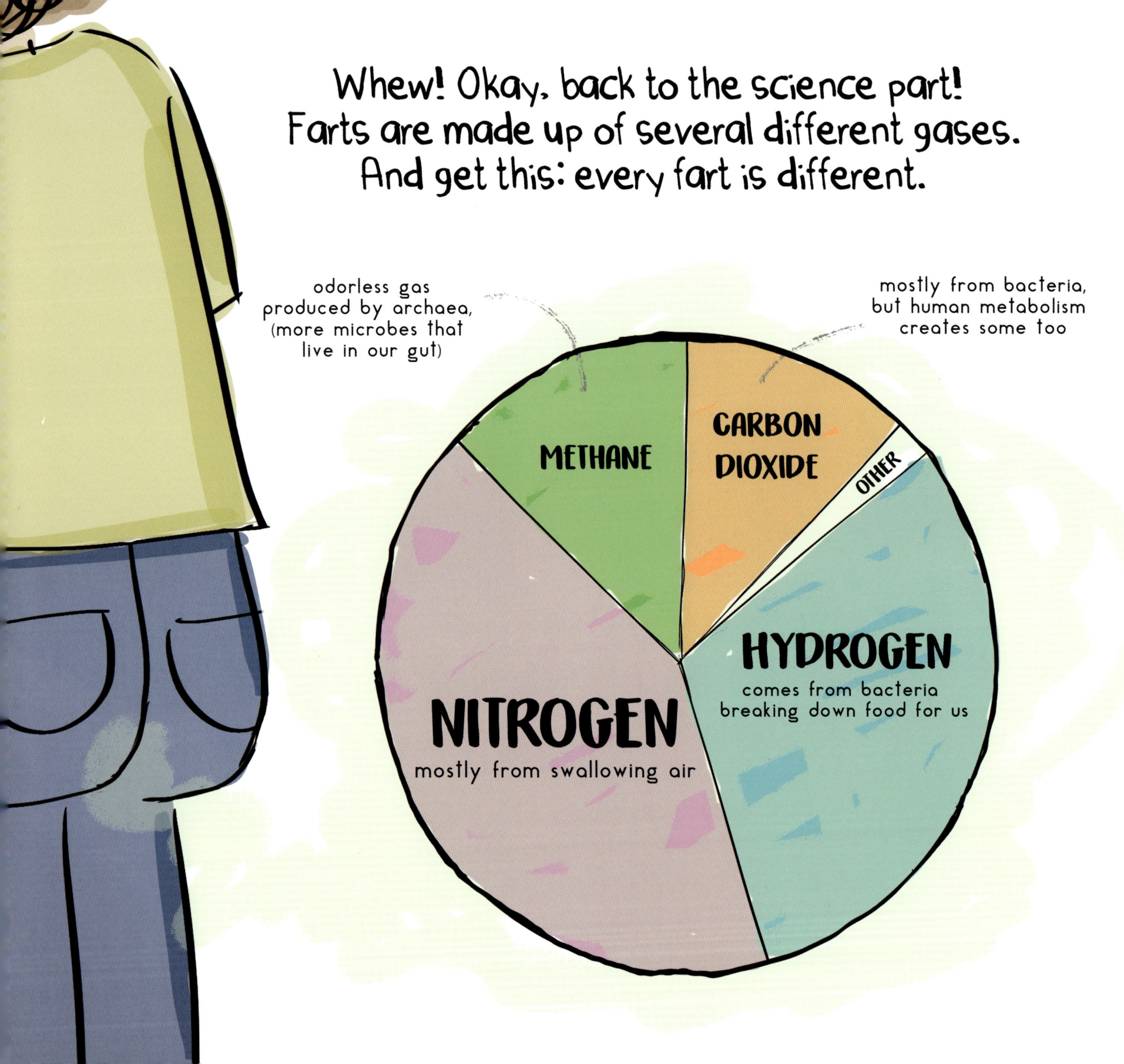

odorless gas produced by archaea, (more microbes that live in our gut)

mostly from bacteria, but human metabolism creates some too

METHANE

CARBON DIOXIDE

OTHER

HYDROGEN
comes from bacteria breaking down food for us

NITROGEN
mostly from swallowing air

Most farts are made of the same ingredients, but how much of each gas can vary wildly based on who's farting, what they ate last, and how long ago they ate it.

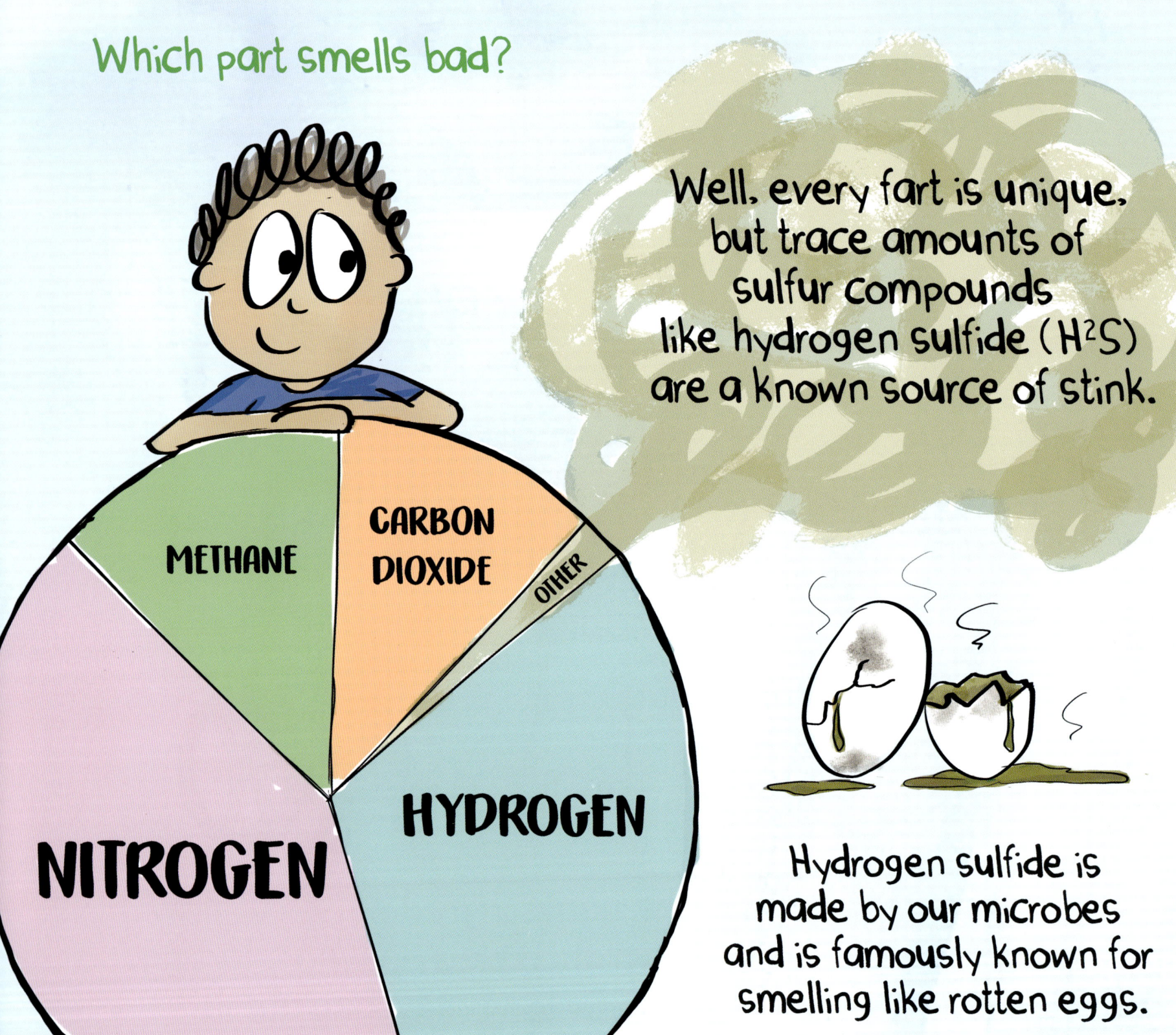

Which part smells bad?

METHANE

CARBON DIOXIDE

OTHER

NITROGEN

HYDROGEN

Well, every fart is unique, but trace amounts of sulfur compounds like hydrogen sulfide (H²S) are a known source of stink.

Hydrogen sulfide is made by our microbes and is famously known for smelling like rotten eggs.

Most people pass about a liter of gas daily and fart ten to twenty times a day!

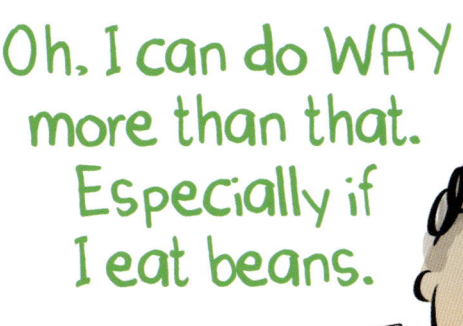

Oh, I can do WAY more than that. Especially if I eat beans.

Oooh! Yes! And I know WHY beans give you more farts!

It's because our stomach and small intestine only have the tools to break down simple sugars and starches.

Easy-to-digest foods are made of simple sugars that our body can easily take apart.

stomach

But fibrous foods like beans, broccoli, cabbage, or brussels sprouts are much more complex and harder to break apart.

small intestine

Fibrous foods are made of stuff like complex carbohydrates, which are more difficult to take apart!

This means fibrous foods pass through most of our digestive system without being used for energy . . .

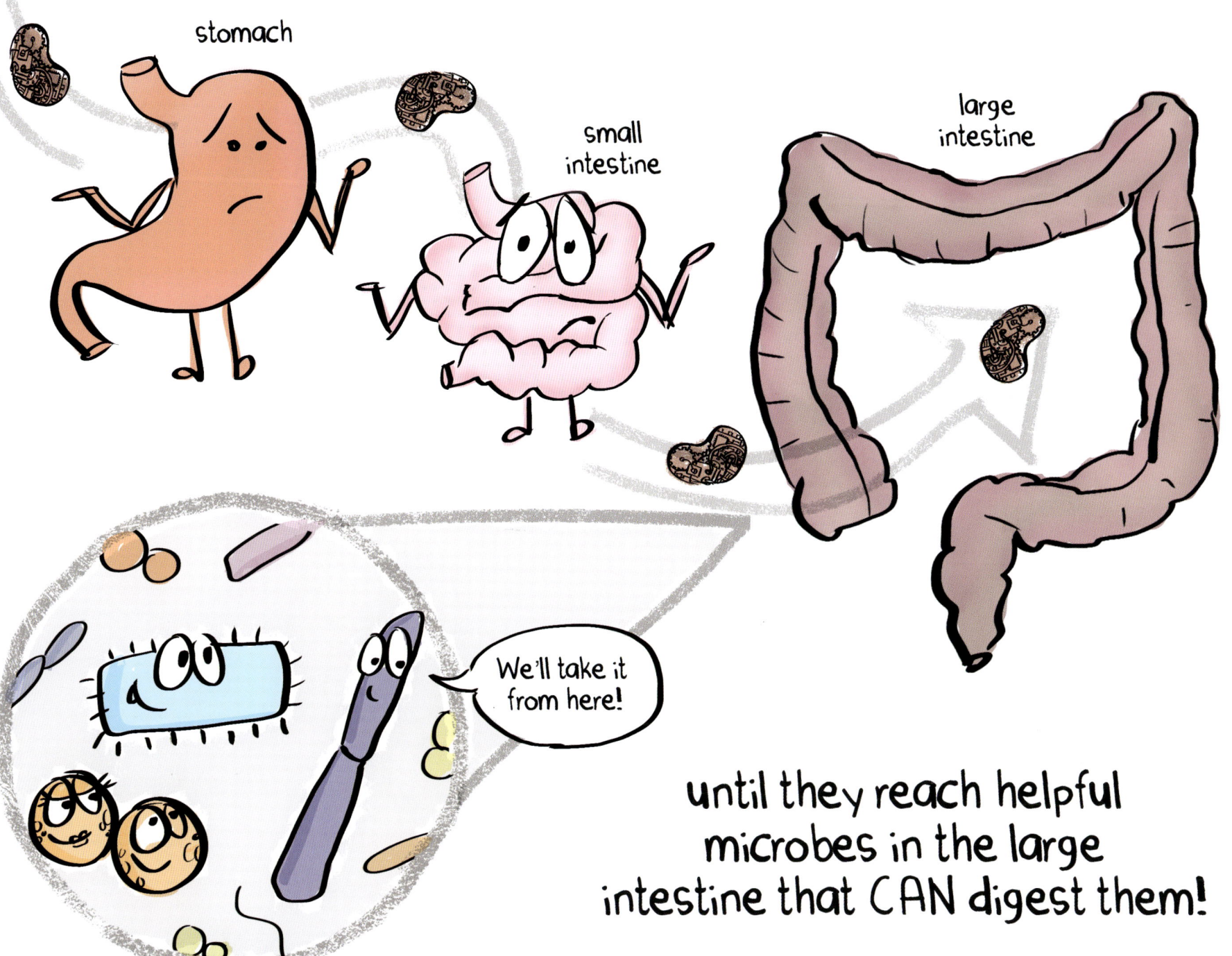

stomach

small intestine

large intestine

We'll take it from here!

until they reach helpful microbes in the large intestine that CAN digest them!

Our gut is home to trillions of microbes, and they have the tools to break down even the most fibrous of foods.

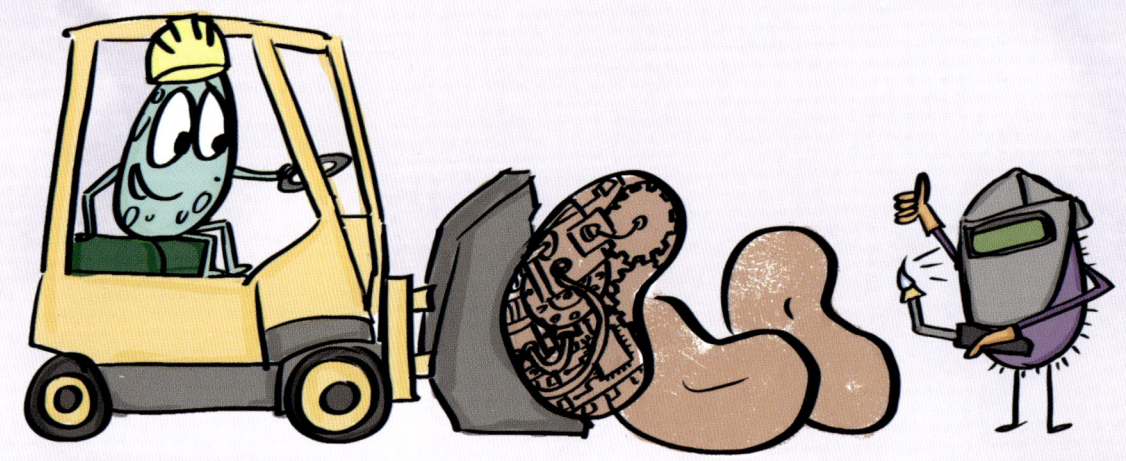

When these microbes chow down, they also release all sorts of helpful stuff our bodies can't make on their own (plus gas).

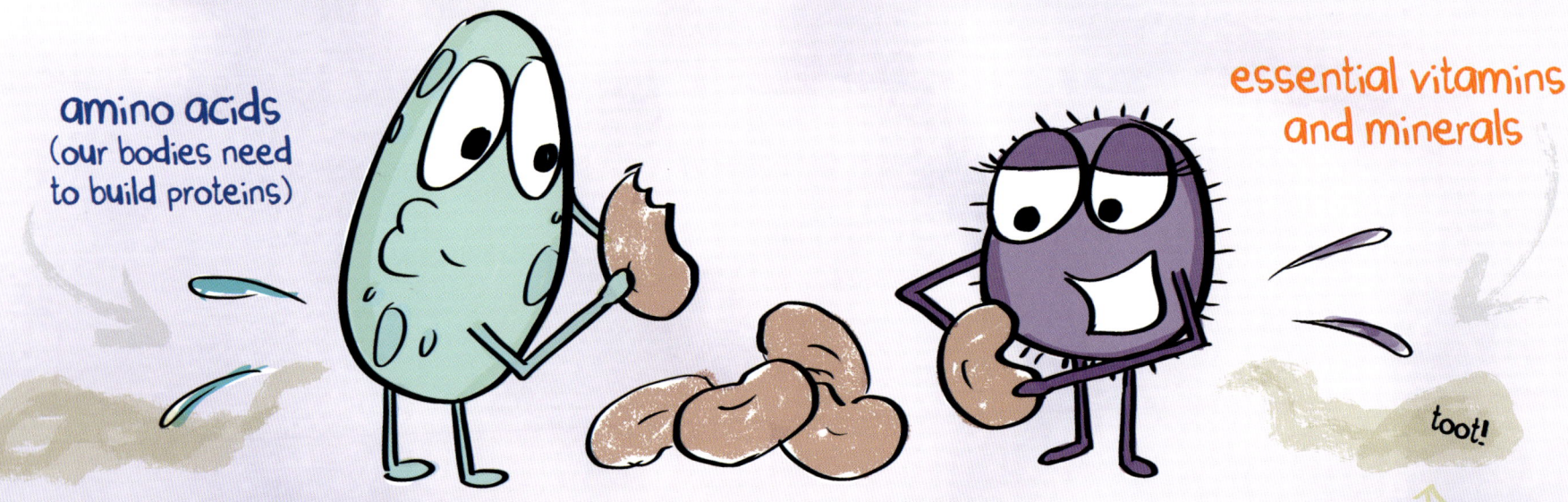

amino acids
(our bodies need
to build proteins)

essential vitamins
and minerals

toot!

So our microbes get a snack, and
we get important vitamins (and also gas)!

Termites are famously flatulent. Their woody diet means lots of complex fiber and sugars to break down—and that means lots of farts.

There are about one thousand pounds of termites for every person on Earth—so those farts add up!

With 445 million tons of farting termites around, it's no wonder termite farts are said to be responsible for 1 to 3 percent of global methane emissions.

Hilariously, farts are also used against them!
Baby beaded lacewings stun their termite
prey by farting on them.

Great shot!

Thanks. Mom!

Lacewing farts contain a special toxicant that paralyzes
termites so the larvae can chow down. It only works on
termites and is powerful enough to take out six at once!

My farts are
also deadly
weapons.

Oh. I know.

Ocean creatures fart too! Manatees can control their buoyancy with farting. And herring use their farts to communicate with other fish in their school.

While most mammals fart, cows, horses, camels, zebras, and elephants are some of the more notably flatulent ones.

Whew! So, as I was saying . . . birds don't fart! They don't have the same gut microbes we do.

Plus, they digest food super quickly, and poop very frequently (sometimes every five to ten minutes), so there's really no time for gas to build up.

Not farting is an option?!

Not for most mammals.

Sloths don't fart! But they still accumulate lots of gas with their super-slow digestive system. If their body didn't have a way to deal with all that gas, they could get really sick, maybe even explode!

So instead of farting, sloth gas gets absorbed by their intestines and put back into their bloodstream.

From there, it's sent to the lungs, where they can exhale it out. (Thankfully, this fart breath doesn't stink!)

It sounds weird, but our bodies do the same thing!

The rear exit is closed. You'll have to take the stairs.

large intestine

hydrogen gas

One study says our large intestine sends up to half of the hydrogen gas in our intestines (aka pre-farts) out through our breath—instead of out the other end.

People and animals that aren't able to fart can have problems . . .

Gas pains and stomach cramps happen when humans aren't able to pass gas through farting or burping.

When fish like the Bolson pupfish can't pass gas, the trapped gas makes them float to the surface, where they can be easily spotted by predators!

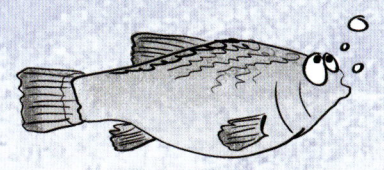

Why not? You just told me: farting is a natural and fascinating by-product of digestion that helps keep our bodies functioning in a healthy balance.

Wow, you were really paying attention.

Yup! And now I'm feeling the fart love.

Me too!

You're welcome.

Fascinating Facts on Flatulence

Making a fart book is a lot of fun. I had an excuse to talk about farts for months on end (for science, of course!).

In the process, I read lots of books and scientific papers. Scientific papers are how scientists and researchers share the findings from their experiments so that people can learn from them, fact-check them, and even build on their findings. Since we're always learning more, there are always interesting new papers to read! The papers I read for this book discussed what science is learning about farts, what gases they're made of, and all the microbes that get involved in the process.

This book would not have been possible without the enthusiastic help of Dr. Austin Campbell. He's an incredibly knowledgeable researcher on this subject and even wrote some of the scientific papers I read! He also posed really fun questions like this one: "Sauropod dinosaurs (the big ones, like Brontosaurus) played the same ecological role that gassy herbivores like cows do today—eating the most fibrous plant matter. It's very likely that they also relied on gut microbes to digest it. Can you imagine how many farts a seventy-ton Argentinosaurus must have produced?!" See what I mean? He's a super-cool dude.

Reading scientific papers was sometimes hilarious too. In one paper, the subjects (the people scientists were collecting farts from) were asked to eat a lot of pinto beans to make sure they'd fart a lot (haha!). Another paper described that farts were collected inside of "gas-tight Mylar pantaloons"—aka shiny balloon undies that collected farts! HAHA!

I hope this book makes you more curious about the fascinating ways your body makes energy and gets rid of stuff it doesn't need. Maybe I'll be reading one of YOUR scientific papers someday!

Where to Learn More:

Does It Fart?: A Kid's Guide to the Gas Animals Pass by Nick Caruso and Dani Rabaiotti, illustrated by by Alex G. Griffiths

It Takes Guts: How Your Body Turns Food into Fuel (and Poop) by Dr. Jennifer Gardy, illustrated by Belle Wuthrich

Science Comics: The Digestive System: A Tour Through Your Guts by Jason Viola, illustrated by Andy Ristaino